TAXI CAB

BY ALEX SUMMERS

Rourke
Educational Media
rourkeeducationalmedia.com

*Scan for Related Titles
and Teacher Resources*

Before & After Reading Activities

Teaching Focus:
Concepts of Print: Have students find capital letters and punctuation in a sentence. Ask students to explain the purpose for using them in a sentence.

Before Reading:

Building Academic Vocabulary and Background Knowledge
Before reading a book, it is important to set the stage for your child or student by using pre-reading strategies. This will help them develop their vocabulary, increase their reading comprehension, and make connections across the curriculum.
1. Read the title and look at the cover. *Let's make predictions about what this book will be about.*
2. Take a picture walk by talking about the pictures/photographs in the book. Implant the vocabulary as you take the picture walk. Be sure to talk about the text features such as headings, the Table of Contents, glossary, bolded words, captions, charts/diagrams, or Index.
3. Have students read the first page of text with you then have students read the remaining text.
4. Strategy Talk – use to assist students while reading.
   - Get your mouth ready
   - Look at the picture
   - Think…does it make sense
   - Think…does it look right
   - Think…does it sound right
   - Chunk it – by looking for a part you know
5. Read it again.

Content Area Vocabulary
Use glossary words in a sentence.

driver
horn
meter
signs

After Reading:

Comprehension and Extension Activity
After reading the book, work on the following questions with your child or students in order to check their level of reading comprehension and content mastery.
1. *What does a taxi driver use a cell phone for? (Summarize)*
2. *What does the meter in a taxi cab tell you? (Asking Questions)*
3. *Did the pictures help you understand what riding in a taxi cab would be like? (Text to self connection)*
4. *What do you do at the end of your taxi ride? (Asking Questions)*

Extension Activity
Be Your Own Taxi Cab Driver! With a few friends, pretend you are a taxi cab driver and one by one let your friends ride in your pretend taxi cab. Don't forget to do all the things the driver in the book does!

Table of Contents

Catch a Ride

Ready to go!

How will I get there?

I know! I will take a taxi cab. The taxi **driver** pulls over.

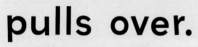

driver

On the Road

He says, "Where to?"

"The zoo," I say.

Parts of a Taxi

He turns on a **meter**. The meter tells me how much my ride costs.

$ FARE $ EXTRAS

1- FARES / TIME
2- EXTRAS / DATE
3- TAXES / DATE
4- DIST
5- PAID DIST
6- TRIPS
7- CALIBRATION

3.50   0.50

HIRED

RATE 1

HIRED   TIME OFF   EXTRAS   RATE

meter

141

I sit in the back seat. *Honk, honk!* The driver beeps the **horn**.

HONK! HONK!

horn

The driver uses a cell phone to map our way and talk to other drivers.

24 km

150 m

Taxi cabs can be any color. Many are yellow or black.

Every taxi cab has a number. Many taxi cabs have **signs** on the top.

sign

Hooray! I am here.
The driver says,
"Five dollars, please."

I pay him and get out. Zoo time!

Picture Glossary

 **driver** (DRYE-vur): A driver is someone who drives a vehicle.

 **horn** (horn): A horn is a device that gives a signal by making a loud noise.

 **meter** (MEE-tur): A taxi cab meter shows how much money per mile you will be charged.

 **signs** (sines): Signs tell people about a business or service.

Index

Websites to Visit

www.learn4good.com/games/driving.htm

www.knowledgeadventure.com/games/crazy-taxi

www.androidappsgame.com/taxi-car-games-for-little-kids

About the Author

Alex Summers enjoys all forms of transportation.
Especially if they are taking her to places she has
never been or seen before. She loves to travel,
read, write, and dream about all the places she
will visit someday!

Meet The Author!
www.meetREMauthors.com

Library of Congress PCN Data

Taxi Cab / Alex Summers
(Transportation and Me!)
ISBN 978-1-68342-161-0 (hard cover)
ISBN 978-1-68342-203-7 (soft cover)
ISBN 978-1-68342-230-3 (e-Book)
Library of Congress Control Number: 2016956590

Rourke Educational Media
Printed in the United States of America,
North Mankato, Minnesota

Also Available as:

© 2017 Rourke Educational Media

www.rourkeeducationalmedia.com

Edited by: Keli Sipperley
Cover design by: Tara Raymo
Interior design by: Rhea Magaro-Wallace
Photo Credits: Cover: ©leezsnow; ©zagar; Page 5a, 6, 22:
©michaeljung; page 5b: ©Oleksander Perpelytsia; page
5c: ©Nerthuz; page 5d: ©tarasov_vl; page 7, 9: ©andre-
ser; page 11: ©Fabio Lavarone; page 13: ©bizoo_n; page
15: ©Rostislav_Sedlacek; page 17: ©viewfinder; page 19:
©MikeDotta; page 21: ©baranozdemir; page 22: ©Lya_Cattel